If you don't have anything nice to say, don't say anything.
Just make a crude gesture.
3

Relatives are like bad pennies. You can shove 'em into snack machines, but it won't do you any good.

Remember, it's not whether you win or lose. It's how many cheap shots you get away with.

Keep a bright outlook!
Maybe today will be the day the accordion is declared illegal!

You can't fight city hall.
You can get a cab to
to drive by real slow
while you egg 'em,
though.

I believe good fences make good neighbors.

You never know when you'll need to buy a hot watch.

14

If a tree falls in the forest__
It better not be while I'm
making a pit stop.

I have a surefire way to feel better when I get the flu.
I give it to as many other people as I can!
Makes me feel a lot better!

If you can't stand the heat,
go in my kitchen.
It's a pretty safe bet
I won't be cooking.

18

You know, if I were the last person on Earth...
That would be just fine with me.

When Someone I Know
is down on their luck.
I always try to help
them out.

"There's the door."
I say, "Get out."

You can't teach
an old dog new tricks.

Luckily, the new mailman
wears the same uniform.

Some people have questions about whether or not to kiss a blind date. Not me. I kiss 'em off about 7:30.

I believe everything happens for a reason.

Usually the reason is that somebody messed up.

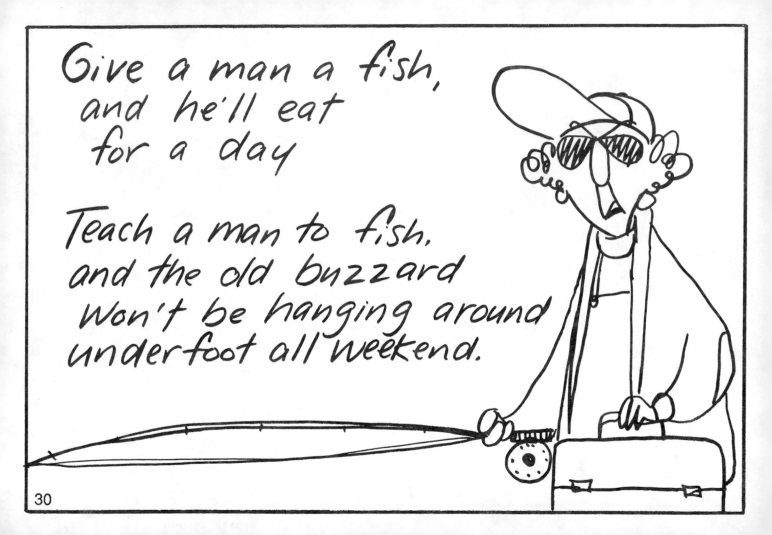

Give a man a fish,
and he'll eat
for a day

Teach a man to fish,
and the old buzzard
won't be hanging around
underfoot all weekend.

Ah, picnics! The perfect combination of noisy kids, relatives, insects and questionable potato salad!

With age comes beauty. Wisdom, and the ability to make a loud honking sound when you blow your nose.

I always try
to take things one
day at a time.

Today I took a
handful of pens,
a floppy disc and
a ream of paper.

37

Sometimes I like hidin' in a pile of leaves and jumping out to scare passersby.

Other times I just like sitting on a park bench to scare passersby.

41

I love baseball!

Any sport that makes spitting and scratching acceptable is OK by me.

After all is said and done...
Beat it! What are you hanging around for?

47

I enjoy walking for exercise. A couple of times through my neighbor's flower garden usually does it.

I like to think of each day as a new mountain to be climbed. a new river to be crossed...

A new neighbor to be mooned.

52

This is the year I finally do something with that extra room where the junk collects.

Close the door and pretend it's not there!

When you really want something in life, go after it!

For example, every time I get on the bus, I sit at the driver's elbow and pester him to let me drive.

When Charities come
for my unwanted Cast-offs
I always give them
the same thing.

My ex's address.
If they want him,
they can go pry him
out of the recliner
themselves.

An apple a day keeps
everyone away
if your aim is
good enough.

Nothing beats a day at a theme park!

Except maybe a blowout in rush-hour traffic on a busy freeway.

The answer, my friend, is moonin' in the window. The answer is Moonin' in the window.

I've written a Country
and western song.
It's called,
"Mamas, Don't
Let Your Babies Grow
up to Ride Their Stupid
Bikes Across My Lawn."

I love All-You-Can-Eat restaurants, or, as I like to call them, All-You-Can-Stuff-Into-Your-Purse,-Your-Tote-Bag,-Your-Hat-and-a-Plastic-Lining-Sewn-Into-Your-Bulky-Coat restaurants.

You know what they Say: "It's not over till it's over!" Wow - wonder how long it took 'em to figure that one out!
THE END

WRITTEN BY:
Chris Brethwaite,
Bill Bridgeman, Bill Gray,
Allyson Jones, Kevin Kinzer,
Mark Oatman, Dee Ann Stewart,
Dan Taylor, Rich Warwick
and Myra Zirkle.

Other books from
SHOEBOX GREETINGS
(A tiny little division of Hallmark)

FRISKY BUSINESS: All About Being Owned by a Cat.
THE WORLD ACCORDING TO DENISE.
DON'T WORRY, BE CRABBY: Maxine's Guide to Life.
EVERYTHING YOU ALWAYS WANTED TO KNOW ABOUT STRESS...but were too nervous, tense, irritable and moody to ask.
40: THE YEAR OF NAPPING DANGEROUSLY.
RAIDERS OF THE LOST BARK: A Collection of Canine Cartoons.
THE MOM DICTIONARY.
WORKIN' NOON TO FIVE: The Official Workplace Quizbook.
THE OFFICIAL COLLEGE QUIZ BOOK.
WHAT...ME, 30?
STILL A BABE AFTER ALL THESE YEARS?
YOU EXPECT ME TO SWALLOW THAT?: The Official Hospital Quiz Book.
THE COLLEGE DICTIONARY: A Book You'll Actually Read!
THE GOOD, THE PLAID, AND THE BOGEY: A Glossary of Golfing Terms.
THE FISHING DICTIONARY: Everything You'll Say About the One That Got Away.
THE DAD DICTIONARY.
THE GRANDPARENT DICTIONARY.
THE CHINA PATTERN SYNDROME: Your Wedding and How to Survive It.
THE HANDYMAN DICTIONARY: A Guide for the Home Mess-It-Up-Yourselfer.
STILL MARRIED AFTER ALL THESE YEARS.
CRABBY ROAD: More Thoughts on Life from Maxine.